The Pope and Contraception

CHATTO
CounterBlasts

Brenda
MADDOX

The Pope and Contraception

The Diabolical Doctrine

Chatto & Windus
LONDON

Published in 1991 by
Chatto & Windus Ltd
20 Vauxhall Bridge Road
London SW1V 2SA

A CIP catalogue record for this book
is available from the British Library

ISBN 0 7011 3741 X

Photoset in Linotron Ehrhardt by
Rowland Phototypesetting Ltd
Bury St Edmunds, Suffolk
Printed in Great Britain by
St Edmundsbury Press Ltd
Bury St Edmunds, Suffolk

Acknowledgements

For help in preparing this pamphlet I would like
to thank, in London, the International Planned
Parenthood Federation, the Catholic Central
Library and the Catholic Truth Society; in Dublin,
the Irish Family Planning Association; in the United
States, Catholics for Free Choice. Also Martin
Albrow, John C. Brook, Christine Donahy, Theresa
Finney, David Lodge, the late Edith Murphy,
Frances Perrow, Sunetra Puri and Holly Rae
Zellweger.

Two books on theology were essential reading:
Contraception: A History of the Church's Teaching
by John Noonan (Harvard University Press, 1965,
revised; 1986) and *On Human Life: An Examination
of Humanae Vitae* by Peter Harris and others (Burns
and Oates, 1968). An elegant and entertaining ex-
position of the transformation in the Church's
teaching on sexual morality is David Lodge's novel,
How Far Can You Go? (Penguin, 1981).

If the possibility of conceiving a child is artificially eliminated in the conjugal act, couples shut themselves off from God and oppose his will.

John Paul II, Chihuahua, Mexico, 11 May 1990

The relevant Popes

Pius XI: born 1857; elected 1922; died 1939
Pius XII: born 1876; elected 1939; died 1958
John XXIII: born 1881; elected 1958; died 1963
Paul VI: born 1897; elected 1963; died 1978
John Paul I: born 1912; elected 26 August 1978;
                died 29 September 1978
John Paul II: born 1920; elected 16 October 1978

THE HOUSE IS still there, shaded by the maple trees that line Main Street in my home town. Not one of the grandest of the old colonial houses, but spacious by European standards: yellow clapboard with white trim, porch roof supported by the Doric columns with which the early settlers proclaimed their New England was really a new Athens.

It was not the kind of house in which most of the Catholics in the town lived. Later arrivals by two centuries, they settled, and built their church, on the outskirts. Indeed, the man of that house was not a Catholic, but his wife and children were. 'Mixed marriage' was a phrase that carried a great deal of meaning in Massachusetts in the 1950s. An uneasy feeling came over me when I used to pass the place on my way to school, for I knew that the wife inside 'practised birth control'.

My mother had told me, to impart information rather than disapproval. She had been widowed in her mid-twenties and paralysed a year later by spinal meningitis. Housebound in a wheelchair, she found in stories of her friends' marriages a glimpse of the world she had lost.

All of us in my grandfather's house where we lived were Catholics, but of the Italian persuasion. No little fonts of holy water in the bedrooms, as our Irish neighbours had; no Sacred Hearts of Jesus bleeding over the sideboard. Yet Catholics all the same, going regularly to Mass, confident in God, the power of prayer and eternal life. My mother offered the tale of her friend simply as a case study from the annals of Catholicism. The wife suffered from a bad heart. No more babies, said the doctor.

'So what does she *do?*' I asked. I had learned the Church's teaching along with the facts of life. Pleasure in sex was quite acceptable – after marriage – but only under two conditions: no contraceptives should be used and the wife must never say no. (The possibility of the husband pleading a headache was unknown in our philosophy.)

'She uses something,' my mother said knowledgeably. 'When she goes to confession, she fights with the priest. She tells him – she's French and very frank – "If my husband doesn't get it from me, he'll get it from somebody else." The priest scolds her for committing a mortal sin and tells her to stop. She promises to try, goes to communion the next day, then doesn't go to confession again for a long time.'

Oh. That was why this woman, known to be devout, was seldom seen at the communion rail.

The dilemma was as clear as it was insoluble. You could not go to communion in a state of sin. You could not say no to a husband without losing him to another woman. You could not have another baby without dying and leaving your children motherless. Tough. That's the way it was. Protest was as useless against the laws of the Church as against the laws of physics. Water will never run uphill.

Today I cannot see that quiet house without thinking of the terrible war within, month after month, year after year: husband versus wife, wife versus priest, life versus death. Terrible and point-less. What a needless addition to the sum of human misery the Catholic Church's teaching against 'arti-ficial' contraception has been.

But that was in another country and, besides, surely the old Church is dead?

Catholics today will tell you that, since the Second Vatican Council's reforms of the 1960s, they follow their consciences, not the Pope. They reject the teaching of *Humanae Vitae* (*Of Human*

3

Life), in which Pope Paul VI in 1968 reaffirmed the Church's ban on artificial contraception. That papal encyclical, they point out, was not delivered *ex cathedra* and did not have the status of infallible dogma. Catholics, every bit of evidence suggests, use contraception to the same extent as the rest of the population does. They do not fear the priest. 'Nobody goes to confession any more,' an American friend told me – a pronouncement confirmed by a Notre Dame University survey a few years ago which reported that the custom of monthly confession was disappearing among American Catholics.

As for the infamous *Humanae Vitae*, David Lodge, in his witty novel of Catholic change, *How Far Can You Go?*, declares it 'a dead letter to most of the laity and merely an embarrassing nuisance to most of the clergy'.

If only it were so. Those who practise their Catholicism in the comfort of Western Europe or North America are well-positioned to write off Paul VI's aberration. They can read what they like and buy what they like. They can shop around for a sympathetic confessor with whom to converse once or twice a year about the state of their soul. Millions around the world are not so lucky.

Around the globe the Church's ban on artificial

contraception is a virulent force for ignorance, repression and suffering. The Church's conservative hierarchy, bolstered by the equally conservative Catholic medical professions and the right-wing political organisation Opus Dei, are hard at work to stop the spread of family planning and sex education. By their efforts they are hampering attempts to control soaring population growth. By their opposition to condoms, they are contributing to the spread of AIDS.

This Catholic doctrine causes more misery than does apartheid. There are only 21 million black South Africans but nearly one billion Catholics, the world's largest religious denomination. Hundreds of millions of women lack even the basic information to space and limit their children. Women do want contraception. Where they can get it, they use it. According to the World Fertility Survey of the Population Crisis Committee in Washington, DC, contraceptive practice in the less-developed world has risen by 10 per cent to 20 per cent in a decade. Yet these countries lag far behind the industrialised world in the methods available.

Contraceptive ignorance goes hand in hand with a high incidence of maternal mortality. In the Congo, where there is next to no contraceptive practice, the rate is 1,000 maternal deaths per

5

100,000 live births, while in Britain, where 83 per cent of married women practise contraception, the comparable rate is 1.8 per 100,000.

In Mexico, a Catholic country suffocating under the weight of its runaway population, the government has defied the Church. Its contraceptive clinics and campaigns advertising the virtues of small families succeeded between 1977 and 1989 (with vasectomies and contraceptives but without legal abortion) in driving down the rate of growth in its birth rate from 3.7 per cent to 1.9 per cent. But families of ten or more are still common, and the average number of children per couple – 3.4 – is a long way from the 1.67 per couple Mexico has set as a target for the end of the century. To achieve this, four-fifths of all Mexican women would have to find the courage to defy their priests and, in many cases, their husbands.

 It must not be overlooked that even in the sophisticated, industrialised world the Church's doctrine hangs like a cloud over the lives of millions of practising Catholics. David Lodge, in his novel, describes them as Catholics who 'continued to believe the Pope's word was law and disobeyed with a residual guilt that they were never able to lose completely'.

I am not among them. I did not stay Catholic

long enough to be discomfited by *Humanae Vitae*. Halfway through my undergraduate years at Harvard – after endless reading, talking late into the night, even making spiritual retreats, I saw my faith slide off like an outgrown skin. Suddenly I realised that I believed in none of it – God, the soul or life after death, let alone the finer details like original sin, the Virgin Birth and the Resurrection. Apostasy was painful but once done, done. I still wince at the phrase 'lapsed Catholic', which suggests something left at the dry cleaner's which you may call someday to collect. I did not lapse. I walked out. I am an *ex*-Catholic. Granted that I have not yet passed the deathbed test, I cannot imagine ever going back.

But belief is not shrugged off easily, and the institutional power of the Church is vast. Its policies affect millions who never pray to the Virgin Mary. In many regions of the globe it wields an institutional influence disproportionate to its numbers of adherents. In Burkina Faso (formerly Upper Volta), for example, Catholics constitute only 9 per cent of the population but run 50 per cent of the hospitals and schools. In such places women have small opportunity to choose between their conscience and the Pope.

The Second World suffers along with the Third. The Church and the pro-life movement have been quick to rush into the breach opened by the collapse of communism. Communist regimes in Eastern Europe made abortion easy. It was cheaper than contraception (especially if, as in the Soviet Union, performed without anaesthetic). It was often the only form of family planning available. Now the Church is leading the fight to repeal abortion and to prevent family planning and sex education from taking its place.

The campaign has already succeeded in Poland, where 95 per cent of the population of 38 million is Catholic. For years the Communist Party, in unholy alliance with the Catholic Church, refused to subsidise any programmes of family planning. The consequence was that Poland, next to Ireland perhaps the most devoutly Catholic country in Europe, had a rate of sixty to seventy abortions for every 100 births, many of them performed on teenagers. This has given Poland a total of about 600,000 abortions a year, nearly four times as many as in Britain.

In October 1990 Poland's parliament took the first step and repealed the abortion laws which had been in effect for thirty-four years, yet, under the new conservative Catholic ethos in sway, there is to be no finance, either, for public contraceptive clinics. What will happen to all the unwanted babies? The teeming orphanages of Ceausescu's Romania, where both abortion and contraception were banned in the drive to increase population, give some hint.

The Church's influence is particularly malevolent in the Catholic Third World. For all the priests who sympathetically dispense contraceptives to overburdened mothers in the slums, the Catholic hierarchies are conservative and powerful, strongly supported by the conservative medical professions.

Argentina has no family planning programme at all. The government in Honduras tried to introduce sex education in the schools; the hierarchy put a stop to it. In the Philippines, the president, Mrs Corazón Aquino, subordinating her own devout Catholicism to the reality of the burgeoning population of 60 million, half of them under fifteen, assigned a greatly enlarged budget to family planning. She had to contend with Bishop Jesús Verla of Sorsogón, chairman of the Philippine Bishops' Commission on Family Life, who sent out a pastoral letter to his colleagues, warning them against the government's immoral new birth-control programme: 'protect our people from the contraceptive onslaught', the bishop said.

In Peru, where the population is set to rise from 22 million in 1990 to 30 million by the turn of the

9

century, the government has offered free family planning advice and devices to all who want them. Yet the Archbishop of Lima has warned from the cathedral pulpit that women using them run the risk of Hell. Undeterred, the Peruvian president, Alberto Fujimori, retorted, 'We don't want a country populated by children feeding themselves from garbage dumps.'

Then there is Ireland, Western Europe's own Third World country, with the highest birth rate in the European Community. Catholic countries with a worldly Mediterranean cast of mind have managed to have their faith and their small families too. Italy's total fertility rate – the average number of children born to women of childbearing age – is lower than Britain's. But Ireland, with a stern Jansenist form of Catholicism, a theocratic Constitution written under the Church's influence and an historic fear of depopulation, had staunchly set its face and laws against the modern tide, until the election of a liberal feminist barrister, Mary Robinson, as president in November 1990. The Constitutional bans on divorce and abortion were recently reaffirmed by popular referendum, even if statistics show that its citizens do not practise what they preach. For years Irish women by the thousands have travelled to Britain for abortion. Now, says the Irish Family Planning Association, the IFPA, a new generation has grown up, which wants only two to three children and is relying on contraception, vasectomy and sterilisation to achieve this limit. It remains to be seen whether Mrs Robinson, who saw her victory as a triumph for Irish women, can use her largely ceremonial office to reduce the Church's power over Irish society.

Ireland did not legalise contraception even for married couples until 1979, after vigorous campaigning by Mrs Robinson, and even then only on a doctor's prescription. More recently, it has relented to the extent of allowing the sale of non-medical contraceptives (spermicides and condoms) to people over eighteen in chemists' shops (if the chemists are willing: a conscience clause allows them to opt out), in family planning clinics and in doctors' surgeries. But nowhere else. Police stopped the IFPA from selling condoms in a Virgin shop (even though Ireland has the highest incidence of the AIDS virus in the EEC. The association was fined £500 for breaking the contraception law.

The Irish medical establishment has so recoiled from the controversies surrounding contraception that it largely leaves to the IFPA, a private charity, the task of instructing undergraduate medical students in the theory and practice of family planning.

Yet Irish girls, like Polish girls, are not immune to the modern world. Illegitimacy, once almost unheard of in Ireland, is, according to the latest available figures, running at 9.6 per cent of total births. Of Irish girls who get pregnant, 42 per cent have no experience of using contraceptives. The entire nation has had experience, however, of the price of ignorance. The 'Kerry Babies' scandal in the mid-1980s brought to light a glimpse of the extent of the dark practice of infanticide – the last resort of a desperate girl and, in that case, her mortified family.

All this misery has been inflicted by a verbal nicety. 'Artificial' birth control is against God's law. 'Natural' methods are permissible even though they require the highly artificial aid of a therm-ometer and graph paper, or a woman probing her private parts for mucus (the Billings method) to try to assess the stage of her monthly fertility cycle.

That this judgement has been handed down by aged celibate men who have not been in bed with a woman since they were weaned is obscene. In-deed, it seems almost like an act of vengeance – a sentence delivered by one sex against the other. Those who refuse to alter it may believe the punish-ment not undeserved. Is there not evidence from the Highest Source that it was a woman who introduced sin into the world?

To the non-Catholic, the underlying objective of the ban on birth control is obvious: to make more Catholics. To many women, the object is equally clear: to allow male society to retain its control over women. The wish to keep women in their place is found in traditional societies around the world, combined with an enthusiasm for large families. One goal serves the other. A woman at home with a lot of babies will stay out of trouble: fecundity serves as a chastity belt, if not as a contraceptive. Around the globe campaigns to promote condoms meet with strong prejudice; a husband assumes his wife has been unfaithful if she dares suggest them. The President of Uganda, Yoweri Museveni, for one, has said that promoting condoms would encourage promiscuity.

Behind the wish for control is the dread of the force of unleashed female desire. It lies in the Irish song, 'Sure 'tis the women are worse than the men'. It lies in the fear of women priests. In one of his more misogynist actions John Paul II has instructed bishops that women and girls should no longer be allowed to serve as readers or to assist in the distribution of communion.

Get back, Unclean Temptress! Your role is to

serve men and to bear children, not to disrupt the social order with your insatiable appetites!

Whatever the motives for denying women contraceptives, the penalty women pay is high. Half a million a year die in childbirth. Of these 99 per cent, according to the World Health Organisation, are in the least developed countries. There, childbirth and its complications are the leading cause of death among women of reproductive age.

'Women'? The average age at which a Third World female bears the first of her seven children is fifteen. Girls giving birth at fifteen or under have five to seven times the risk of death of older mothers. Perhaps the Pope should tuck this statistic into his sermons as he processes around the world preaching 'self-control according to methods which respect nature'.

Repeated pregnancies with insufficient recovery-time threaten children as well as mothers. Forget the prostitution and abuse that engulf unwanted youngsters when they hit the streets of their *favelas* and slums to try to fend for themselves. Those children are lucky to have reached the age of two. The space between births and the mother's level of education are the biggest factors in a child's chances of surviving the precarious first year.

The perverse doctrine deserves to be called dia-

bolical: fiendish, wicked, atrociously cruel. It is a
threat to the planet. World population, now 5.2
billion, will stabilise within a century at 10 billion,
according to the United Nations Population Fund
– but only if more people use family planning.
The alternative, with uncontrolled growth, is
14 billion.

But global statistics veil the harsh reality of the
Church's determination to deny women reliable
birth control. The victims are individuals, suffering
alone, their stories known only through hearsay.
One documented case, however, appeared in the
Irish Times on 2 September 1983.

Sheila Hodgers died of cancer in Our Lady of
Lourdes Hospital in Drogheda on 19 March 1983.
She had first gone to the hospital in August 1981
with a tumour on her breast. Like many Catholic
wives in Ireland, Mrs Hodgers, who had two children already, had been taking the contraceptive pill
as a 'cycle regulator'. Following a mastectomy
for a deep tumour, however, she was taken off
the pill, for sound medical reasons. Hormones
in the pill can reactivate cancer of the breast or
womb.

So can pregnancy. Doctors usually advise waiting
for two years after a mastectomy before contemplating another baby. Mrs Hodgers was offered

15

anti-cancer tablets but no substitute contraceptive. She became pregnant. Shortly after the diagnosis, in September 1982, Mrs Hodgers returned to Lourdes Hospital and, because of danger to the foetus, was taken off the tablets she was receiving for cancer. Soon she began to experience severe back pains. It seemed that the cancer had re-appeared but the hospital refused to take an X-ray because of the possible harm to the unborn child. Abortion was, of course, out of the question.

Untreated, the cancer tumours spread rapidly. By Christmas she could neither stand nor walk and was allowed home only for a brief visit. Back in the hospital she was in severe pain. As her husband, Brendan, told the *Irish Times*, his wife was not even given painkillers. 'I went to see Sheila one night and she was in absolute agony. I could hear her screaming from the front door of the hospital and she was on the fourth floor.'

The baby, a girl, two months premature, was born on St Patrick's Day, 1983, and died immediately. Two days later Mrs Hodgers died of tumours of the neck, spine, legs, liver and ribs.

O birth, where is thy victory?

The Hodgers case was a hard one, even for Ireland where there is wide difference of opinion on the application of Catholic teaching to medical ethics. A senior cancer therapist thought the use of chemotherapy and radiation on pregnant women was justifiable in religious terms. But radiation renders a woman sterile. It was the hospital's policy that no woman was ever sterilised. 'But,' said a senior consultant in the North Eastern Health Board region, 'you won't get any doctor or consultant to say that publicly or they would be fired. They're under the Bishop's contract, in fact they are under the highest religious authority in the country, Cardinal O'Fiaich.'

But sterilisation would not have been necessary had Mrs Hodgers been offered the common everyday protection of a Dutch cap or an intra-uterine coil.

No method of contraception is foolproof. Condoms and caps can puncture. Pills can cause thrombosis. Intra-uterine devices (my own least favourite in the 'artificial' stable) can cause heavy bleeding. Even tied fallopian tubes sometimes let through the odd sperm, as surprised parents of my acquaintance will testify.

The Church and the pro-life groups argue that their approved methods of natural family planning – notably the so-called Billings method – work as well as any of the 'artificial' methods, with the added advantage that no product need be bought or supplied. The method requires teaching women to distinguish between the moistness of the vulva at mid-cycle, when ovulation is taking place, and the comparative dryness of the other, non-fertile days. 'When you are wet, a baby you will get' is the couplet the Billings method uses to help women to remember (although its catchiness may lose something when translated into Spanish or Gujarati).

The Billings claims are upheld by the World Health Organisation, which confirms that the failure rate of this and other rhythm methods is no higher than the rest. Statistically speaking, this could well be true. However, Father Sean McDonagh, who ran a mission on Mindanao in the Philippines, has written in his *The Greening of the Church*, 'In eight years not a single family, even those in daily contact with the sister-nurse, has been able to apply these methods successfully.'

In fact, natural methods may be no less reliable than artificial methods, but they are no more reliable either. They are entirely unsuited to women at two important stages in their reproductive lives: when they are nursing and when they are in, or approaching, menopause. When periods are irregular or absent, the wet-dry test becomes meaningless.

For all the drawbacks of modern methods, there

is no doubt at all that their regular use heavily reduces the chances of conception. The true cause of 'failures' is hard to ascertain; anything can contribute, from faulty manufacture to human fluster or deliberate design. None the less, I'm willing to bet that if you could identify those women who, before intercourse, unfailingly insert a diaphragm lubricated with spermicidal cream, you would not find many pushing a pram.

The natural methods are a useful tool in the task of holding down soaring birth rates, but in themselves they are not enough. Every method is needed, especially modern contraception. The only hope of holding world population down to 10 billion by the year 2100 lies in helping women in the developing countries to cut the number of children they bear by half. And soon – before the year 2005.

None of this means that the Catholic Church is the *cause* of the population crisis. Rapid growth is scarcely confined to Catholic countries: China comes to mind. Improved maternal and child care, the 'green revolution', better sanitation, the use of pesticides, the lack of a world war: all contribute to a rapid increase in babies surviving to reproduce themselves. And the cure lies beyond contraception. The 'demographic transition' from high to low birth rates occurs in societies where parents have lost the ancient fear of infant mortality and have some confidence that, even if they have only two children, these are likely to survive until the parents' old age. It lies also in an increase in literacy and in opportunities for women to work outside the home, which in turn brings the most essential change of all: women deriving their sense of personal worth from something other than the number of children they bear.

But the Church is hampering the cure, by placing obstacles in the way of women limiting their families and, not incidentally, by perpetuating the ethos which lowers women's self-esteem.

It is a disaster for the planet that contraception has become linked with the controversy over abortion. This is not a CounterBlast against restrictions on abortion. Let others fight that fight. The Church's ban on contraception affects many many millions more. Contraception and abortion are totally different. Abortion is a misery, a traumatic invasion of the body, shunned by many couples with no religious belief whatsoever, who prefer to live with their 'mistake' rather than to abort it. I count it my good fortune never to have had to make the decision. Contraception, in contrast, is a routine act of hygiene, performed over thirty years or more of a woman's life. The difference is like that between having a tooth extracted and brushing your teeth. But don't take my word for it.

'Abortion is entirely different from contraception,' the Papal Commission on Population and Birth Control reported to Pope Paul VI in 1966, 'because it concerns a human life already in existence.'

The logic should be clear to everybody, even those like me who cannot accept that a cluster of cells fourteen days old can in any way be called 'a human being'.

Aha, says the pro-lifer. Women are lazy, especially the promiscuous ones. They use abortion as a means of contraception.

This heartless view can only come from people who have never witnessed the frenzy of a woman hoping that she is not pregnant. She thinks of nothing else. Desperate *not* to have to make the trip to the abortion clinic (or worse), she runs to the lavatory hour after hour, even in the middle of the night, to see if reprieve has come.

The merciless pro-lifers deride family planning and sex education as 'anti-life'. How can any wife who wants to space her children be classified 'anti-life'? Why not relabel her efforts 'pre-life'?

The deliberate confusion goes on, in rich and

poor countries alike. The well-funded International Right to Life movement (in which conservative American Catholics make common cause with the kind of fundamentalist Protestants who were burning down Catholic homes two generations ago) knows no frontiers. In South America the Alianza Latinoamericana Para la Familia appeals for donations thus: 'The Latin American family is under great pressure today. Abortion, population control and misguided sex education programmes are taking their toll.' In Britain, Family and Youth Concern boasts of its role as 'a body which does much good in countering the propaganda of the "family planning" industry and the sex industry in general'. Organisations, like these and the powerful Human Life International run by Father Paul Marx in Gaithersburg, Maryland, circulate videos and pamphlets whose titles speak for themselves: *The Population Hoax*, *The War Against People*, *The Anti-Life Conspiracy* and *Birth Control: Why are They Lying to Women?*

To the woman who is pregnant and does not want to be, British Victims of Abortion offers counselling, healing, understanding – and that's all. The Society for the Protection of the Unborn Child offers prams, nappies, maternity clothes – everything but the means to avoid needing them all again.

What a travesty of common sense. If you hate abortion, you should want to prevent its cause.

With one voice, these organisations prattle pro-natal propaganda about 'the resourceful earth'. The planet could feed 40 billion, they say. And so it could – as long as the 40 billion did not all want to keep their food in refrigerators. Or live in clean, uncrowded homes, educate their children to minimum standards of literacy and numeracy and enjoy the peace and beauty of undeveloped wilderness. These laudable motives for family limitation are dismissed – by John Paul II foremost – as selfishness and materialism.

Increase and multiply. The more the merrier. Unimpeded intercourse, says the Pope, is the duty 'couples owe to God'.

The pro-life alliance has succeeded in spreading the Big Lie: that contraception causes abortion. The Revd Jerry Falwell says: 'The argument that making contraceptives available to young people would prevent teen pregnancies is ridiculous. That's like offering a cookbook as a cure to people who are trying to lose weight.'

Wrong. That's like saying that wearing seatbelts causes road accidents. Even the papal commission in 1966 did not go that far, and pointed to evidence that abortions are more numerous in places where contraception is neglected. Recent Eastern European experience confirms this observation, as does that of The Netherlands, where there is virtual abortion-on-demand and easy access to contraception as well. The result is the lowest abortion rate in Europe.

The success of this guilt-by-association PR trick has had grave consequences for world population control. The United States has withdrawn all support from the UN Population Fund and the International Family Planning Federation, the primary sources of contraceptive aid to the Third World. President George Bush is more worried about maintaining his anti-abortion stance and placating American Catholic bishops than about contributing to the $7.6 billion a year the World Bank estimates is needed now to put a brake on the growth in population. That sum is four times present world spending.

And it is not only the American government which is shy of the pro-life lobby. The National Academy of Science has reported that American research laboratories, world leaders in every other field of science, now lag decades behind Europe in contraceptive research. And, following pressure from its shareholders, the American Telephone and Telegraph Company withdrew its annual donation of $50,000 from the Planned Parenthood Federation of America.

But let's face it. Why should those on the moral Right differentiate between abortion and contraception or sex education? Their interest is to keep the wages of sin what they have always been: birth.

They do not hesitate to say so. Digby Anderson, for example, the *Sunday Times* columnist, told the International Conference on the Family in Brighton in July 1990 that girls should be kept in fear of the consequences of promiscuity. Illegitimate children should be made to suffer the shame of bastardy. 'Stigma is necessary for an orderly society,' Mr Anderson said. 'Ridicule, gossip, social exclusion are the glue which keeps society in order. We need more of that unpleasantness in our society.'

That was British understatement. The American Catholic writer and champion of family life Phyllis Schlafly has made herself clearer: 'It's very healthy for a young girl to be deterred from promiscuity by fear of contracting a painful, incurable disease, or cervical cancer, or sterility, or the likelihood of giving birth to a dead, blind, or brain-damaged baby (even ten years later when she may be happily married).'

25

Society, as Margaret Thatcher once said, is made up of individuals. The Catholic Church's contraceptive ban is not only a global threat; it is an insult to human dignity. It invades the privacy of husband and wife and weakens the very bond which makes happy marriage the bulwark of human society.

Back, briefly, to my home town. On Sunday evenings my mother, her wheelchair bundled into somebody's car, went to meet a group of women friends. They sewed and knitted, they ate very sweet desserts, and they talked unguardedly. Both Protestants and Catholics were in the group. (The town was like Belfast in that everyone knew everyone else's religion. Unlike Belfast, it had no sectarian schools and everyone had friends from both religions.)

One of the wives was always making them all laugh. She was young, pretty, very naive – Polish, wouldn't you know? With the circle she had shared the trauma of her wedding night, when she had not known how to tell her new husband her secret shame: she could not sleep unless there was a chair by the bed. On another evening she had a different tale to tell. Father D—— had said the most terrible thing to her in confession. What it meant she did not know, but she could not possibly repeat it.

'Tell us!' cried the others. 'It can't be that bad if a priest said it!'

She could hardly begin. 'He said . . . He asked me . . .' and then it came out. 'He asked: "Do you ever spin the seat?" Wasn't that *awful*!'

She went bright pink, no doubt flooded with visions of what her confessor suspected she and her husband got up to in their bed with the chair beside it.

The Protestant women were flummoxed. They could make no sense of it. But one of the Catholic wives could. 'He didn't say "spin the seat", silly! He asked: "Do you *spend the seed?*" They always want to know that.'

The interpretation was correct. Pope Pius XI had laid on parish priests the specific duty of cross-examining married people in the confessional about their contraceptive practices. Withdrawal, *coitus interruptus*, was on the Church's blacklist along with the rest.

Of course, the wish to thwart the consequences of joining the sexes' congruent parts is as old as civilisation. John Noonan, in his superb *Contraception: A History of the Church's Teaching*, gives ample evidence of the ancients' ingenuity. The Egyptians in 1900 BC made female pessaries of pulverised crocodile dung in fermented mucillage. Soranos of

27

Ephesus, who practiced in Rome between AD 98 and 138, in his authoritative *Gynaecology*, recommended pessaries of pomegranate seed mixed with peppermint juice and honey. The Romans, not content with various potions and pessaries, also favoured 'post-coital exercises'. Jumping up and down, they believed, made it harder for sperm to reach their destination.

For much of the present millennium, Avicenna's *Canon of Medicine*, written in eleventh-century Damascus, was the main European textbook. Avicenna gave useful recipes – a douche of three pints of sweet basil steeped in water – and exercises as well. After intercourse, he said, the woman should take seven to nine jumps backward. She could also try sneezing (to make the sperm slippery).

Against these common practices were ranged two millennia of anti-contraceptive doctrine, through Augustine, St Paul and St Thomas Aquinas to nineteenth-century theology. All derived from the few words in Genesis (38:8–10) about the wretched Onan who cast his seed upon the ground. Never mind that Onan's intention was to avoid intercourse with his dead brother's widow, as commanded by the custom of the levirate, for the purpose of keeping property within a family. The Church and its Protestant counterparts glossed these lines to forbid any male ejaculation from which the sperm did not enter the vagina.

By 1909, as more sophisticated forms of the male condom and female cap were becoming available, the Vatican had begun to vent its hostility. Cardinal Arthur Vermeersch, a Belgian theologian, acknowledged that the issue of contraception could cause domestic discord and alienation from the sacraments. No one should be surprised. 'Why should it be astonishing that conjugal chastity, like all the Christian virtues, claims its martyrs?'

For all that, no Pope had ever formally spoken out on the subject of contraception. Pius XI settled that with *Casti Connubii* (*Of Chaste Spouses*). A magisterial distillation of two millennia of anti-contraceptive doctrine, it concluded with the resounding declaration that remains the Church's teaching today:

Each and every marriage act [quilibet matrimonii usus] must remain open to the transmission of life.

Thus the diabolical doctrine is only sixty years old. Two developments prompted *Casti Connubii*. One was the falling birth rate across Europe following World War I; France, for example, with a sagging population, passed a law in 1920 forbidding contraceptive propaganda and also adopted pro-growth

policies which endure in the generous family allow-
ances paid to large French families to this day.
The other, more likely the actual trigger, was the
Anglican Church's reversal of its opposition to birth
control. Anglican bishops, in 1908 and 1920, had
voted to condemn contraception. But on 14 August
1930, after a decade in which the work of Marie
Stopes and the family planning movement had
made a great impact on British social thinking,
the Lambeth Conference reversed its position and
decided that 'where there is a clearly felt moral
obligation to limit or avoid parenthood, the method
must be decided on Christian principles'.

Pius XI swiftly moved to distance the Roman
Church from Anglican woolliness. *Casti Connubii*
appeared on 30 December 1930. It merely reaffirmed the Church's teaching – but with greater
force and authority than ever before. *Casti Connubii*
did stop short of an *ex cathedra* pronouncement. It
went far enough, however, to impale the Church
on the hook where it remains, brushing aside all
the arguments for contraception: 'no reason can
make congruent with nature what is intrinsically
against nature'.

Over the centuries the Church had come to
accept that sexual pleasure was part of God's plan.
It had moved away from the harsh Pauline 'better

to marry than to burn' view that marital intercourse for non-procreative purposes was a regrettable necessity to avoid temptation. Instead, it had come to see the sexual act as the medium of expression for the love of husband and wife, therefore having a secondary function nearly as important as the first. This recognition raised a whole thicket of moral problems which the church's theologians eagerly tackled.

Is it permissible for sterile couples to have intercourse? – (Yes). May sterile couples use contraceptives? – (No). How far should a wife go to resist a husband bent on contraception? – (To the same extent that she would resist rape, but not to the point where her life is threatened). Is sex in any non-procreative position condoned? (Never).

The sessions in which the cassocked scholars sat around a table discussing the relative iniquities of oral sex, anal sex and *amplexus reservatus* (intercourse without orgasm; pleasure without end) do not bear thinking about.

In 1951 an important adjustment to the teaching came from Pius XII, who had succeeded to the throne in 1939. In a policy statement known as his *Address to Italian Midwives* he conceded that a married Catholic couple might be morally justified in wishing to space the births of their children.

They might even, for reasons of genetic handicap and the welfare of the existing children, want to prevent more altogether. In other words, he condoned the rhythm method – also known as the Safe Period, 'natural' family planning or Vatican roulette.

For many, the Church had exposed the fatal flaw in its argument there and then. If it were morally permissible to try to outwit God's procreative plan by using a calendar and thermometer, how could it be wrong to use rubber or cream or simple withdrawal for the same purpose?

Discontent, disillusion and unhappiness swept the Catholic world. In the Lodge novel, dutiful 1950s Catholic couples earnestly give the rhythm method a try, and are rewarded with a spate of unplanned pregnancies and a Down's Syndrome child. 'In practice,' says the narrator, 'the Safe Method was so unreliable that many couples wondered if it hadn't been approved only because it wasn't safe, thus ensuring that Catholics were restrained by the consciousness that they might after all have to pay the traditional price for their pleasure.'

Then came the 1960s and a new Pope. John XXIII, a man in his eighties, turned out to be no 'caretaker Pope' but a vigorous, imaginative reformer. He called for an *aggiornamento*, which meant, roughly speaking, dragging the Church into the light of the modern world. The Second Vatican Council (the first, in 1870, had proclaimed the dogma of infallibility) brought together representatives of the entire worldwide Church, to re-examine every aspect of its teaching and ritual. Simultaneously with the council, John XXIII established a Papal Commission on the Family, Population and Birth Control.

By its very existence the commission acknowledged the totally changed climate of opinion on population. In place of pre-war fears of decline, there was a new anxiety about the world's ability to provide a decent life for its rising billions. What is more, there were new pharmacological techniques for making analogues to the hormones which control female ovulation. In 1960 the US Food and Drug Administration had approved a progesterone pill as a contraceptive. Where did 'The Pill' fit into the theological framework? Where, for that matter, did the theories of Freud, Jung and Kinsey? Sexuality was, more than ever, seen not as a base urge but as the normal expression of a healthy personality, one which priests denied themselves as a deliberate sacrifice in order to serve God. Besides, the nature of marriage had clearly changed. In centuries past, marriages were quickly broken by the death of one or other of the partners. With new longevity, a promise made 'till death us do part' was expected to last for fifty or sixty years.

John XXIII well understood the magnitude of the task. He determined that his commission should have strong laical representation. Along with theologians, he appointed demographers, gynaecologists, psychologists, specialists in the sociology of marriage, and, daringly, even some actual married couples. Then, in 1963, in the sixth year of his reign, to the incalculable loss of the human race, he died.

His successor, Pope Paul VI, was Cardinal Montini of Milan, a thin, cautious traditionalist who had previously served as the Vatican's pro-Secretary of State. The new Pope inherited an open debate on birth control which seemed to take as its premise that the traditional teaching was obsolete. And pleas for change poured in – from outside the Church – one hundred Nobel Prize-winners wrote to the Pope on the need for population control – and from within. From Bombay, the Catholic Archbishop Thomas Roberts gave an audacious and widely printed interview in which he openly repudiated the Church's teaching. The typical villager, said Archbishop Roberts, already had more children than he could feed and not even a light to comfort him at night – nothing, except the love of his wife. It was unreasonable to ask such a man to exercise sexual restraint. In Britain Dr John Rock, a Catholic, published *The Time Has Come* - the time to stop looking at narrow issues such as whether the pill caused temporary 'sterilisation' and begin instead to look at marital sex in the context of the entire marriage.

Meanwhile, sessions of the Vatican Council were rocked when a succession of speakers, including several venerable Cardinals, rose to warn the Church of its 'negative attitude towards human love' and also of the danger of binding Catholic consciences with contentious doctrines unsupported by the certainty of divine law.

Word then began to leak out that the population commission was taking a dangerously reformist line. In 1964 Paul VI, like Franklin Roosevelt packing the Supreme Court, diluted the laical representations on the commission by adding a number of orthodox theologians from various parts of the world, where the local bishops were not eager to see the traditional teaching changed. Even so, towards mid-May 1964, when a vote was taken, the size of the progressive majority favouring a change was surprising: fifteen to four. And the commission

35

continued to tilt towards reform. Its final report, delivered to the Pope on 28 June 1966, recommended that the traditional teaching against contraception be abandoned.

In its report, the commission reminded the Pope that the Church's moral teaching on conjugal relations had been the subject of conflict since the beginning of the Church and that 'the Church is itself necessarily and continually in pilgrimage.' To its heritage of revealed truth, the Church was constantly amplifying its teaching accorded to man's stored experience. In essence, the report said that new scientific knowledge about reproduction and sexuality made it now possible to see, as was not possible in the early days of the Church, that reason required married couples to use contraceptives to ensure the spacing of births and the proper education of their children.

Read today, the commission's words, allowing for the inevitable stickiness of pious prose, are pretty plain. 'Therefore, the morality of sexual acts, between married people takes its meaning first of all and specifically from the ordering of their actions in a fruitful married life, that is one which is practised with responsible, generous and prudent parenthood. It does not then depend upon the direct fecundity of each and every particular act.'

The Church could afford to change with the times, without in any sense breaking with its past, just as (here there was a dig at St Paul) it had moved away from the views of 'some authors who even used expressions which depreciated the matrimonial state'. No one was to be shocked 'if we advocate the regulation of conception by using human and decent means, ordered to favouring fecundity in the totality of married life'.

The reasons for the *volte face*? 'Social changes in matrimony and the family, especially in the role of the woman; the lowering of the infant mortality rate ... [and] a changed estimation of the value and meaning of human sexuality and of conjugal relations'. Besides, the Church had to respect the views of the Catholic faithful around the world, views which fervently held that 'condemnation of a couple to a long and often heroic abstinence, as the means to regulate conception, cannot be founded on the truth'.

How should couples decide what form of contraception is right for them? 'By common counsel and effort, [taking] into account both their own welfare and that of the children, those already born and those which may be foreseen. They will take into account both the material and spiritual conditions of the times as well as their state of life.'

37

Of course, of course. The International Planned Parenthood Federation could not have put it better.

Paul VI rejected the report. The blow came on 25 July 1968, with the appearance of the heartbreaking encyclical, *Humanae Vitae*. The Pope thanked the commission, but: 'The conclusions which they came to the Pope cannot accept ... some of their proposals went much too far away from what the Teaching Church has always said.' In other words, the Church could not be seen to change its mind. Paul restated the command of Pius XI: 'every act of marriage must, in itself, stay destined towards the chance of human procreation'.

In case there were any doubt, he amplified: 'All actions are forbidden which stop the natural effect of any marriage act, whether done before the act or during it, or after it is over.'

In a section entitled 'What is Allowed' he permitted 'therapy for some organic trouble though it may stop conception'. In 'What is Forbidden' he excluded 'sterilising either sex permanently, or for a while'. Those are the words which two decades later denied Sheila Hodgers radiation treatment and chemotherapy.

Tough? Oh, yes. Just like my Catholic girlhood. The teaching might sound hard, the Pope conceded, even impossible. Married couples should pray and seek the sacraments, 'for then they will not grow depressed because of human weakness'. He sympathised, but he was helpless. 'It is for God, and not the State, to regulate relations for a couple.'

Shamelessly, *Humanae Vitae* concluded with an appeal to scientists to get the Church out of the pit it had dug for itself. Paul VI implored them to find 'a way at once both sure and lawful, for regulating birth by use of natural rhythm'.

And there we stand.

Humanae Vitae is unreal. It reeks of inexperience. The concept of 'each and every act' excludes any awareness of the times when sex is a happy continuum and the distinction between one 'act' and the next disappears, or of other times when the conjugal *coitus* is interrupted by the child at the door whining 'I can't sleep!' It is a celibate abstraction imposed on the real world.

Any hope that the advent in 1978 of the first non-Italian Pope in nearly 500 years, the charismatic, politically sophisticated Cardinal Wojtyla of Warsaw, would bring a more realistic approach to the problems of modern marriage faded fast. The present Pope has brought a combative, media-manipulative approach to the old harsh doctrine. He is deaf to those who plead with him that a less self-assured stance on difficult issues would be more pastorally sensitive. He seems to delight in telling those who are suffering most that there is no hope: homosexuals cannot be good Catholics, women cannot be priests, priests cannot marry, AIDS victims may not use condoms. 'Love faithfully,' he tells them.

For some Catholics, *Humanae Vitae* freed them to correct the Pope. 'The error of *Humanae Vitae*,' according to Lionel Keane, a London parish priest and frequent speaker at Westminster Cathedral, was to classify what was 'natural law', or self-evident truth, to St Thomas Aquinas in thirteenth-century Bologna as the 'constant teaching' of the Church, and therefore unalterable. Instead, in Father Keane's analysis, the criterion of 'constant teaching' should be applied only to revealed truth, the word of God. Self-evident truth can be enlarged or modified by science, experience and observation, which is exactly what has happened in the twentieth century to the understanding of human reproductive physiology and psychology.

But informed scholarship has not swayed John Paul II. Nor has intense and continuing criticism from within the Church. The Revd Bernard Haering, former Professor of Moral Theology at the Gregorian University in Rome, and a member of the papal commission on population, sent a letter to his 'Father in Christ' in 1988. After a fulsome bow ('We have many reasons for loving you ... your untiring enthusiasm for justice in peace ...' etc.), Father Haering said he was shattered to learn from a German Catholic journal that only 12 per cent of the faithful under the age of fifty and only 25 per cent of those above were ready to listen to the papal words on sexual morality.

Why, the German thinker asked, is a woman who has already given birth to genetically defective children not morally justified in using artificial methods of birth control 'when what is ultimately involved is maintaining the mutual self-giving of marriage and the bond of loyalty? How can one argue so simplistically? That is not the image of God which Jesus makes tangible and visible for us.'

That was putting it mildly. Other German theologians abandoned tact. In January 1989, in an unprecedented act of defiance, 163 Catholic theologians, mainly from West Germany, attacked John Paul II for scandalous, arbitrary and suffocating extensions to his authority. The 'Cologne Declaration', signed by a group including Professor Hans Küng, who was deprived of his chair of Catholic Theology a decade earlier for his outspokenness, accused the Pope of leading the Church into 'creeping infallibilism' – regarding all its teachings as protected from error, not just those declared *ex cathedra*. Under him, they said, the Church had become fixated on birth control. Catholics should disobey him.

His response was a leader in the Vatican newspaper *Osservatore Romano* (with three asterisks at the end to show that it was authoritative) stating that the Church's teaching on contraception was settled, not a matter for discussion. There followed a fierce encyclical letter on the 'ecclesiastical vocation of the theologian', which in effect told any dissenters – German, American, whatever – to be silent.

Since then rumour has swept the Church that the Pope was contemplating a catastrophe: a new encyclical on morals that would declare the ban on birth control, beyond any doubt, to be the infallible and unalterable dogma. From German progressives came a new declaration, from Tübingen. In it they implored him to hold back from making worse a teaching 'which has been rejected by the overwhelming majority of the Catholic people and the Catholic clergy'. Instead of an encyclical on morals, they said, he should set up a competent commission to investigate the question of papal infallibility in the context of the teaching on birth control.

The Pope is as likely to take their advice as he is to get married.

So where's the rage? The protests? The marches? The leading articles in responsible newspapers? The righteous indignation on *Any Questions*? You will not find them. There are too many Catholic voters, readers, friends. It is not done to criticise other people's religions. Best leave the turbulent priests to fight alone. Besides, what's the point? The Church is not a democracy. The Pope is on his throne for life. Those who would put the world right prefer softer targets like South Africa, nuclear power, and polluted beaches.

It is almost comic the way that political leaders avoid the taboo subject. President Bush declared war on the cocaine industry in South America. But South America has bigger problems: the burden of debt and the need to support a runaway population, half of which has not yet produced its first child. Mrs Thatcher spoke of the need to protect the environment but she dared not agree with Father McDonagh's *The Greening of the Church*: 'How will history judge leaders who refuse to acknowledge the strains which rapidly increasing populations are placing on the earth?'

Both President Bush and Mrs Thatcher trooped

to the United Nations World Summit for Children in September 1990 to discuss ways to stop 40,000 children dying every day, and to reduce malnutrition by half. Emerging, they uttered pieties: Mr Bush, that 'all those children can be saved'; Mrs Thatcher, that 'the family is the best defender of children's welfare'. How refreshing it would have been to hear instead an endorsement of the declaration issued by the 1968 Human Rights Conference in Tehran: 'Couples have a basic human right to decide on the number and spacing of their children and a right to adequate education and information in this respect.'

Of the two, the British leader was freer to be blunt. Britain is a country with a smaller proportion of Catholics, one whose established Church has been committed to family planning for as long as the Roman Church has opposed it. But the Labour Party is no more courageous. It boasts strong family policies, including promises of more day-care and help for single families. But no call for improved sex education. There are too many votes to lose.

A few non-Catholics, to whom all praise, are speaking out. Prince Philip was one of the first. On a visit to the Vatican he raised the awkward question of overpopulation. True, as reported in the *Observer*, the Prince seemed more worried about the planet's wild animals than its slum families. But he did utter home truths on the Pope's home ground: 'There is only a limited quantity of the earth's goods. The more people there are alive on the earth, the greater the demand for them.' He repeated his fears in October 1990 in a BBC documentary, 'For God's Sake?', which itself broke new ground in attacking Catholic policy as a threat to the environment.

There have been others. The Prime Minister of Norway spoke up when the Pope visited Oslo. The *Guardian* newspaper has referred to 'A Church Lost in the Pelvic Zone'. A. N. Wilson has singled out the Pope as his choice of villain: 'an anti-intellectual right-wing bully whom historians will see as largely responsible for the Catholic Church's decline'. Occasionally there is a letter to the editor. In the *Los Angeles Times*, a reader questioned the sincerity of the Pope's pleas for respect for ecology, when 'one word from him could do more to alleviate suffering than all the public and private family planning programmes put together'.

But it will take more than scattered individual voices to counteract the united conservative Catholic front.

AIDS, ironically, may come to the rescue. Some good could come of this plague if it exposed the danger in the papal fundamentalism. On the basis of a sentence in St Paul (Romans 3:8) – 'One should never do an evil directly with the excuse that good will come of it' – the Pope has swept through Africa, where 5 million people are already infected with the AIDS virus and which expects by the end of the century to have 10 million orphans whose parents have died of AIDS – and told them not to use condoms.

In Ouagadougou the Pope declared that youth must 'face the plagues of modern times'. In Ivory Coast, where 700,000 are estimated to carry the virus, he blessed a basilica and said that the way to combat AIDS was with fidelity and family values. In Madagascar he advocated self-control.

Back in Rome, the Dean of the Vatican's John Paul II Institute for Marriage and Family Studies, Monsignor Carlo Caffarra, confirmed that the Pope really did mean 'no condoms'. If a spouse – even a haemophiliac heterosexual infected through a blood transfusion – has the virus, said the monsignor, the couple 'has the grave obligation of total abstinence'. If such abstinence threatened the marriage – through adultery or disharmony – sexual relations might be morally permissible. But under no conditions were they to be protected by condom. Couples, he felt, might prefer to safeguard spiritual good rather than the 'good of life'.

*

This is madness. More should say so. Why does not the Queen speak out, or the President of the Royal Society? It can be done. On 20 October 1989 the *New York Times* pointed the finger at the Church. In a strong editorial, it said: 'Every religion has the right to set its own doctrine without interference. But when the doctrine affects public health, that's everyone's business.' The *Times* went on to question the Vatican's reasoning. For those Catholics engaged in what the Church considers immoral behaviour, 'morality surely dictates the use of condoms in order not to endanger the lives of others'.

More of that, please. The ban on reasoned contraception is not to be borne. Women should parade with placards demanding that the Church give them the most important right of all: to choose not to become pregnant. Those who call themselves 'green' should boycott the largest of the institutions that threatens the environment. Perhaps the public interest now requires Catholic churches to carry a government health warning: 'This religion may endanger your health.'

Can the Church rescue itself? Some dream of a solution through biotheology. If the Vatican could persuade itself that human life did not begin until

47

the fourteenth day after conception, the problem would be solved. After all, biologists agree that a fortnight passes before a fertilised egg reaches the stage of cell division, at which it may split into twins or triplets or more. Theologians agree that the individual soul is immortal and indivisible. Why cannot it be said, therefore, that the soul does not enter until the cell cluster has determined how many individuals it is to make?

A sensible legal escape from the dilemma has been suggested by a philosophy professor from Georgetown University in Washington, D.C. Why not, asked Hans-Martin Saas, adopt a legal definition of 'brain birth' which would parallel the widely Church – could accept that a foetus was entitled to legal protection from the time when integrated brain function began to emerge – then society would have a clear and useful definition of the point where a life could be considered human.

The moment in development to which he referred occurs 10 weeks after conception, when nerve cells which will form the cerebral cortex first become interconnected. If accepted as the beginning of human life, this definition would permit not only forms of birth control that prevents the fertilised egg from implanting in the uterus but the vast majority of abortions.

But there is no need for casuistry. The way out lies through the door that *Humanae Vitae* slammed shut. The papal commission's report on population just needs dusting off. The answers are all there. Married love should be looked at in its entirety, not as a succession of individual acts. Responsible parenthood requires contraception. The thinking of the Catholic faithful in their millions should be respected.

There should be no great difficulty in the Church's changing its mind. After all, it changed its mind on usury.

Sadly, no change is in sight. The nonsense about 'each and every' act of intercourse having to remain unprotected will persist until a new Pope has the courage to stop it. By then the planet will be well on its way to the promised 14 billion people.

But the years roll on. In August 1978 the world was astonished at the selection of timid little Cardinal Luciani of Venice to succeed Paul VI. Cardinal Basil Hume, when he returned to London, dismissed suggestions that they had got the wrong man. 'We have chosen God's candidate,' he declared. A month later God changed His mind. John Paul I was dead. Back to Rome the cardinals went, to choose again.

49

In time, they will be called to this duty once more, and the white smoke will rise again over the cupola of the Sistine Chapel. Let us hope that when it does, it signifies God's choice of a candidate who places love above righteousness, who sees the way out of this senseless abyss and who knows in his heart that the Roman Catholic Church owes the modern world a massive *mea culpa*.

About the Author

The author and journalist Brenda Maddox was born in Massachusetts and took a degree in English literature at Harvard. She has written extensively on women and marriage, and, when home affairs editor of the *Economist*, on Ireland.

Her five books include *The Half-Parent* (a study of stepparents); *The Marrying Kind* (a study of homosexuals in heterosexual marriage) and *Nora: the Life of Nora Joyce*. This widely acclaimed biography of James Joyce's Irish wife published in 1988, winner of the *Los Angeles Times* Book Award for biography and the British Silver P.E.N. award for non-fiction, has been translated into seven languages. She writes a weekly column on media in the *Daily Telegraph* and is now working on a biography of D. H. Lawrence.

CHATTO
Counter*Blasts*

Also available in bookshops now:-

If you want to join in the debate, and if you want to know more about **Counter*Blasts***, the writers and the issues, then write to:

Random Century Group, Freepost 5066, Dept MH, London SW1V 2YY